# Rasp

MW01096541

**Beginner to Pro – Step by Step Guide**

**By**

**Timothy Short**

of monetary gain or other damages which may be caused by following the presented information in any way shape or form.

The following information is presented purely for informative purposes and is therefore considered universal. The information presented within is done so without a contract or any other type of assurance as to its quality or validity.

Any trademarks which are used are done so without consent and any use of the same does not imply consent or permission was gained from the owner. Any trademarks or brands found within are purely used for clarification purposes and no owners are in anyway affiliated with this work.

# Table of Contents:

# The Raspberry Pi 3

The Raspberry Pi 3 is a credit-card sized mini-computer with no movable parts and a large hobbyist community. Within a single-board device measuring less than 3.5 x 2.5 inches are all of the components you need to run a full-fledged desktop operating system. At the very reasonable cost of $35 USD, the Raspberry Pi 3 is a formidable budget computer capable of handling word processing, video streaming, and light video game emulation with ease.

Despite the popularity of a computer that can fit in your pocket and be powered from a cell phone charger, most users prefer to use Raspberry Pi machines for embedded hobby projects. The strong electronics and wide range of interfaces allow neat contraptions such as digital picture frames, model rockets, amateur cell phones/tablets, and even a smart-connected home.

Purchasing a Raspberry Pi 3 will prove to be a smart decision. Whether you choose to use the small technology to create a clever project, or whether you want a portable computer that you can take with you, the Raspberry Pi 3 has the power, interfaces, and functionality to impress you and fulfil your needs.

## RPI 3 Compared

The original RPI computer debuted in 2012 to a decent amount of popularity. The system was severely underpowered compared to the newer model 3, and thus the amount that could be done with the computers was much smaller. It was really only useful as a PC through a text-based command line as graphical desktops were extremely slow. Each iteration of the RPI sought to improve the hardware, and as such the RPI 1A, 1B, 1A+, 1B+, and model 2 polished the hardware, increased specifications, and added new outputs all while staying within the same small form factor. Finally, 2016 saw the release of the RPI Model 3, which brought the greatest amount of improvements while keeping the same price and small size. The device was then truly capable of serving as a computer replacement.

Specifications of the RPI 3 include:

- 1GB of DDR2 RAM. Previous models had as few as 256MB, but 3's amount is ample for running applications. The RAM is faster than older models.
- 1.2GHz, 64-bit ARM processor. Original models started with a 32-bit, 700MHz processor, the RPI 3 offers a significant improvement.
- 4 USB ports. The original models have 1 or 2 ports.
- HDMI output for modern video monitors.
- Micro-SD card slot for data storage.
- 40 GPIO interface pins, providing a plethora of digital engineering functions.

- Built-in Wi-Fi and Bluetooth radios that were previously only available as USB dongles.

As it is evident, the RPI 3 is quite beefy for being so small. If you have followed the hype and news surrounding the surge in single-board, moving part-less, mini-pcs, you will probably know that various alternatives to the Pi exist. While the hardware may be better in competitors such as the Radxa Rock Pro, Banana Pi, or BeagleBone, the community and available help surrounding the devices are significantly less. Should a problem arise troubleshooting your RPI computer, a large community of experienced developers and users will usually be happy to help.

Overall the build quality of Raspberry Pi devices is far greater than that of its competitors too. Furthermore, the Raspberry Pi foundation sells a large number of 1$^{st}$ party peripherals that are built excellently and guaranteed to work with your RPI without issue. Therefore when it comes to SoC (system on a chip) computers, Raspberry Pi computers top the list every time. When considering an integrated project electronic or portable PC replacement pick up the well-received Raspberry Pi 3 computer for a consistent caliber of performance and features.

## Buying an RPI 3

The Raspberry Pi foundation does not actually sell their products directly, rather those looking to purchase an RPI 3 will need to do it through a reseller. There are specific third-party sellers but Amazon or EBay work just fine for acquiring a new device. Buying used is not particularly recommended so make sure that the RPI that you are purchasing is brand new. Furthermore, make doubly sure that you are purchasing an RPI model 3 instead of an earlier one.

In addition to the actual computer you also need a way to power it. The RPI 3 is powered using the micro USB port cable that many Android cellular devices also use, and it is entirely possible you have one lying around. However, sensitive electronics require a clean and constant power, so purchasing a $1^{st}$ party power supply online is an investment that will keep the Pi running more reliably and longer.

Computers are usable bare and exposed (such as how the Pi is a plain circuit board) but many users prefer to enclose their RPI 3 within a case. Third-party sellers have their own custom cases with a variety of colors and styles, but many mini PCs use the same component layout and form factor so it is possible to get cross compatible cases that work well with the Raspberry Pi 3. Cases can protect the Pi from accidental drops or liquid spills to an extent; consider using one for more rugged projects or if you plan to carry the computer around.

To interface with the RPI you can plug in any standard USB keyboard or mouse. Also, due to the RPI 3 containing Bluetooth, there are a variety of wireless peripherals that can be connected once the computer is actually on, but wired connections are always more reliable and easier to set up.

Finally, you need a microSD card to operate the RPI. The mini PC does not contain any onboard storage, so there is no way for the RPI to boot an operating system without a microSD card present. Any microSD card will do, but it is recommended to obtain a Class 10 rated card for maximum throughput and boot speed.

You can purchase parts separately or you should look into buying a Raspberry Pi starter kit which often contains everything you need to get started. The latter is often a better purchase because there are combination deals available when purchasing your rpi3 as a kit. Kits or even sold at some physical brick-and-mortar stores such as Barnes & Noble or Hobby Lobby, so if you're looking to pick up a Raspberry Pi as soon as possible call your local store and ask if they carry the third generation model. It is sometimes cheaper to obtain the computer, all the cords needed, a preformatted microSD card, and a case all in one set rather than buying each part individually.

Conclusively you will most likely purchase your device through an online distributor. Because there are no moving parts the components within it, an RPI 3 will ship through the mail very well. Many of the third-party sellers are located in the United Kingdom but there is no danger in shipping the computer overseas. To operate the system on a chip it will need to receive a stable source of power through a micro USB cable. Even though the cables are abundant because of their use in Android cell phones it is still recommended that you purchase an official power supply to minimize potential issues. And finally a case is not required but they will often come with RPI starter kits and combo deals.

## Setting up the RPI 3

Unpackage your RPI, connect it to a monitor or TV with an HDMI cord, insert a keyboard and mouse, and plug in the power via USB cable. There is no power button on the device, so if there is power flowing through the cable the RPI will turn on automatically. Without an operating system installed in on an SD card, though, the RPI is not very useful at all. If you bought a starter kit or a bundle containing an SD card it probably has an OS on it already. Insert the card before supplying power and the OS will boot.

If you did not purchase a preinstalled microSD card, then you will need to flash a blank SD with an operating system. This means you need a way to plug the card into another computer, either with an SD to USB converter or with a laptop that has a microSD card slot. Insert the card into your internet connected computer, then open a web browser to download an operating system image.

The RPI contains an ARM processor, which limits the number of operating systems it can use. Popular OS choices include Raspbian, Windows 10 IoT, OpenELEC, and Ubuntu MATE. Each OS has a different focus, so choosing one depends on what your computing focus is on.

Beginners will typically install the NOOBS software to a microSD card.  NOOBS is not an operating system- NOOBS is an application that makes downloading and installing an operating system to your microSD card exceptionally straightforward.  For newbies, the process is explained here:

1. Download a copy of NOOBS (https://www.raspberrypi.org/documentation/installation/noobs.md)
2. Extract the zip file
3. Insert and format the microSD card as FAT.  In Windows, you right-click on the device in "Computer" and select "format" specifying the filesystem as "FAT".  All data will be erased.
4. Copy the extracted files to the blank microSD, and finally safely remove the card

Because NOOBS just replaces itself with another OS, you should still understand the different operating system choices for the RPI and choose one for your needs.

Raspbian is an OS built specifically for the RPI.  It is based on Debian, a Linux OS.  Because it is directly supported, Raspbian is usually the best choice of an OS to install.  It can handle general computer tasks such as browsing the web or writing documents, but it also contains programming software for interacting with GPIO pins for hobbyists and DIYers.  An RPI starter kit will most likely contain the newest version of Raspbian (although some contain NOOBS), and typically the

OS provides enough functionality for the average user. Raspbian uses Linux, so those coming from a Windows environment will be slightly confused as to how specifics work, but generally the OS launches common applications graphically just as Windows does.

If in doubt as to which OS to install, definitely try out Raspbian (https://www.raspberrypi.org/downloads/raspbian/).

Windows 10 IoT (https://developer.microsoft.com/en-us/windows/iot) is a trimmed down version of Windows 10 that is meant to be run on minicomputers for DIY projects. Win10 IoT runs "headless", meaning that it runs without a monitor attached. Users are able to upload code to the RPI from another computer. Hobby projects are abundant, as the small size of the RPI is perfect for a variety of uses. IoT is a fast operating system for interacting with hardware, but it is not an OS that is usable for everyday tasks.

OpenELEC is an operating system for media. The popular Kodi application is compatible with OpenELEC, and creating a "smart TV" with an RPI is a highly desired project. OpenELEC is not usually used for desktop browsing functions such as surfing the web because OpenELEC's main features are music and video organization. Those that have a media server can use their RPI to stream media and those that install Kodi can essentially build their own open-source Amazon Fire stick capable of downloading movies and television shows on-demand. Install OpenELEC (http://openelec.tv/) for building a multimedia device.

Ubuntu MATE (https://ubuntu-mate.org/blog/ubuntu-mate-for-raspberry-pi-3/) is another Linux OS that is perfect as a daily driver. The ease-of-use that Ubuntu is known for is integrated with the MATE desktop environment to provide an OS for the RPI 3 that runs very well. Because the RPI models have relatively low specs compared to a desktop computer, most operating systems would simply not run at all. However, Canonical (the Ubuntu company), were able to slim down their desktop experience to work on ARM processors without also removing too many features. Typical OS applications are usable within MATE, such as web browsers, chat programs, video games, multimedia players, and more. Additionally, since Ubuntu serves as the base of MATE, it is also compatible with Ubuntu's ARM software repositories. Besides Raspbian, MATE is an attractive choice for using your RPI as a computer replacement.

Other OS options include:

- OSMC – another media focused OS
- Arch Linux – a minimalist Linux OS for intermediate users
- Pidora – Fedora Linux for the Pi

This next section only applies to the user that is manually installing an OS to the microSD card.  If you put NOOBS on the card, skip the directions below.  However, if you downloaded an OS image continue reading.  Download the image correlating with your chosen OS and insert the microSD card into the computer.  We can now begin the process of writing the OS to the microSD card.

1. Download an image writing tool.  The Raspberry Pi foundation recommends Win32 Disk Imager (https://sourceforge.net/projects/win32diskimager/). Extract and run the .exe file with administrative privileges.
2. Select the drive letter that matches the microSD card. To find it, open up "Computer" and take note of the capital letter that correlates to the microSD drive.  If you select the wrong drive letter, you could potentially erase the hard drive in your computer.
3. Click "write" and the process will begin.  Give it enough time to finish, then close the program and safely eject the microSD card.
- If you use Linux, the process described in this link may help explain how to write an image.

Put the microSD into the RPI and supply power- the computer will turn on and boot into your OS of choice. NOOBS users should plug in an Ethernet cable to give them internet access, as NOOBS requires the network to download your final OS. Choose the OS you want to use from the menu and follow on-screen prompts to install it. For this book, we will be looking at a few of the features present in Raspbian-install it to get going.

No matter whether you wrote the OS manually or used NOOBS to install it, the final booting could take anywhere from 20 seconds to a minute depending on the speed of your microSD, as the entire OS image must be loaded from the card. The console will continue scrolling text as modules and functionality are loaded, but finally, Raspbian will finish booting and hand control over to the user.

# Using Raspbian

Two scenarios arise based on your installation method. Normally a NOOBS installation of Raspbian will boot directly into a graphical user interface, but manual installations of the OS might boot into a text-based terminal. If you see graphics, skip this paragraph. Those used to graphical user interfaces will be very confused initially seeing a text-only interface, because before you can use the mouse there are a few things you must do. You are prompted for a login, and you can use the default username "pi". Then, a password is needed. Enter "raspberry" to authenticate yourself. Mistakes will re-prompt the user for details again, enter the password carefully. After successfully logging in, the terminal will greet you wait for your text input. Linux experts can get right to work with whatever they want, but beginners need to know how to start the GUI. Type "startx" and press enter to start up the "x" application, a program that facilitates graphics on the screen.

Each version of Raspbian is slightly different, but this guide refers to the 2016 "Jessie" release. The screen may look slightly different than how it is described, but the major features are nearly identical. Raspbian Jessie's graphical interface works just like a Windows-based PC, so you have a mouse cursor and icons on the screen to interact with.

The desktop contains icons and shortcuts. Jessie only contains one icon- a wastebasket that works much like the Windows Recycle Bin. Double click icons on the desktop to open them.

The taskbar at the top displays open applications and also has a "start menu" type of functionality from which you can launch more programs. Opening the start menu is done by pressing "Menu" at the very top left. The icon immediately next to it is an internet browser, followed by a file explorer, a terminal launcher, and a few other icon shortcuts. The top right of the screen has options for Wi-Fi, volume, and more.

**Connecting to the Internet**

There are two ways with which the RPI 3 can connect to the internet- either with a LAN cable or with the new built-in Wi-Fi. Physical connections with an Ethernet cable have lower network latency and are undeniable easy to set up. Just plug in one side of the cable to the RPI and then plug the other side into your router or modem. Raspbian will detect the connection automatically and you will gain network access.

Alternatively, you can connect with Wi-Fi. Early versions of Raspbian Jessie did not contain the update that allowed Wi-Fi access. Check the top right corner of the screen on the taskbar.  Besides the volume icon, there should be a Wi-Fi symbol denoted by a signal strength meter.  If that bar is missing you will need to update the software on your RPI.

Plug in a LAN connection for temporary internet access.  On the taskbar click the terminal shortcut to bring up a text interface.  Type "sudo apt-get update", then "sudo apt-get upgrade" to download and install the newest software versions.  Restart the computer to see the Wi-Fi icon (you can now unplug the LAN cable).

Click the Wi-Fi icon and select your network.  Enter a password, if needed, and you will be connected to the internet wirelessly.  Jessie's web browser, Epiphany, is a lightweight application that allows you to surf the web.  Click the start menu button, hover over the "internet" tab, and click "Epiphany Web Browser" to open it.  You can now access websites like you already do on your desktop, laptop, or smartphone.

**Office Productivity**

Raspbian Jessie comes with the free and open source software (FOSS) LibreOffice Suite installed.  LibreOffice is a free program that is meant to be a replacement for Microsoft Office, a product costing well into hundreds of dollars.  The suite comes with a variety of products that have Office counterparts, such as LibreOffice Writer (Word), Calc (Excel), Impress (PowerPoint), Draw (Paint), and Base (Access). Cross compatibility with multiple popular formats such as .doc and .docx make LibreOffice a great choice for writing documents without having to pay for MS Word.

To access any of the products in the LibreOffice Suite from within Raspbian, you must click the start menu button. Hover over the "Office" tab to display every program in the suite. Just click one to launch it and type documents like normal. When saving your work, though, change the file type to something more recognizable and compatible by Microsoft Office users.

## Games

Due to a deal with the game company Mojang, every copy of Raspbian comes with a free copy of Minecraft Raspberry Pi edition. Not fully feature-complete, Minecraft RPI is a stripped down version of Minecraft that is optimized to run on the basic Pi hardware.

Also, the OS has a variety of games written in Python. Tetris, Snake, Match Four, Simon Says, and more are available for fun. Python is a popular programming language preinstalled in Raspbian. You will learn more about Python should you choose to program the RPI, as they are very compatible with each other.

To access the games, access the menu button and hover over the "Games" tab.

**Preferences**

From within the top menu (which is actually called the LXDE menu), the tab "Preferences" contains applications to change various aspects of the Raspbian operating system.

- Appearance – Allows you to change the "theme" (color scheme) of Raspbian. Fonts, mouse cursors, icons, colors, and more can be specifically edited to customize the look and feel of your RPI 3 OS.
- Audio Device – Select an audio device to output sound from.
- Main Menu Editor – A way to customize the main menu of your RPI Raspbian Jessie OS.
- Mouse and Keyboard Settings – Specific options involving your mouse and keyboard, such as sensitivity.
- Raspberry Pi Configuration – This is where you can change your username, password, computer name. The interfaces tab allows you to enable hardware and

software peripherals, such as attached cameras and serial devices. Performance gives you overclocking options, but overclocking will increase the heat output of the RPI and make it unstable so it is not recommended. Lastly, the Localization is a tab for setting time zones, language, and keyboard layouts.

## Accessories

The accessories tab contains shortcuts to other commonly used applications. The "File Manager" is how you see the filesystem on your microSD card and is thus how you edit folders and such. The Windows equivalent is called "Explorer". Other applications include an image viewer, a text editor, and a link to a terminal.

## Programming

As the RPI is meant as a teaching tool, it comes with the Java and Python programming languages installed already. Navigating to the "Programming" tab will preinstall development programs that can be used for programming. The applications BlueJ and Greenfoot facilitate Java programming, while a Python interpreter can be opened with its respective link. Mathematica is a programming language that is used to run Wolfram math programs. The language is highly advanced and usually used in colleges. Lastly, Scratch is a beginner's programming tool. It teaches fundamental programming concepts that will introduce you to the logic involved with writing code.

## Shutting Down the RPI

After done experimenting around with raspbian, you will need to shut down the Pi. There is an entire section on this because of the importance of shutting down the computer correctly. Pulling the power source can potentially corrupt the SD card, so make sure the power is off completely before removing it. Within the LXDE menu, there is possibly a shutdown option. Some versions of Raspbian do not contain this button, so you will have to open a terminal. Type "sudo shutdown –h now" to issue a shutdown command safely. Raspbian will wrap up any activity, shutdown the OS, and leave the computer in a safe state where you can unplug the power source.

# GPIO Pins

One of the most interesting features in a Raspberry Pi 3 is the inclusion of 40 GPIO pins directly on the board. GPIO (General Purpose Input / Output) pins are connections used for building circuits in digital electronics. Each pin that has GPIO function can be set to send or receive a signal to the circuit built on its pin. It is through these pins that so many advanced hobby projects can be made, for you can interface with the Pi with physical sensors and other components. Take for example the following scenario:

You would like to create a thermometer with your RPI 3, but the device does not contain a built-in thermometer. With GPIO pins you can buy a separate temperature thermometer and connect it to the Pi and now it can read temperatures. Take it another step further and connect 3 LED bulbs to the Pi. Now the project can be programmed to light up a red LED when it is hot, a blue LED when it is cold, or a green LED when it is room temperature. The possibilities are nearly endless and only restricted by how creative your imagination is.

Every pin on the Pi is numbered, and some have special purposes. Turning your Pi sideways will orient the pins to correlate with the table below (the GPIO will be at the top right of the board in this orientation).

| Purpose | Pin Row 1 | Pin Row 2 | Purpose |
|---|---|---|---|
| 3v3 | 1 | 2 | 5v |
| GPIO2 (I2C) | 3 | 4 | 5v |
| GPIO3 (I2C) | 5 | 6 | Ground |
| GPIO4 | 7 | 8 | GPIO14 (UART) |
| Ground | 9 | 10 | GPIO15 (UART) |
| GPIO17 | 11 | 12 | GPIO18 |
| GPIO27 | 13 | 14 | Ground |
| GPIO22 | 15 | 16 | GPIO23 |
| 3v3 | 17 | 18 | GPIO24 |
| GPIO10 (SPI) | 19 | 20 | Ground |
| GPIO9 (SPI) | 21 | 22 | GPIO25 |
| GPIO11 (SPI) | 23 | 24 | GPIO8 (SPI) |
| Ground | 25 | 26 | GPIO7 (SPI) |
| NO, NOT CONNECT | 27 | 28 | DO NOT CONNECT |
| GPIO5 | 29 | 30 | Ground |
| GPIO6 | 31 | 32 | GPIO12 |
| GPIO13 | 33 | 34 | Ground |
| GPIO19 | 35 | 36 | GPIO16 |
| GPIO26 | 37 | 38 | GPIO20 |
| Ground | 39 | 40 | GPIO21 |

Note, unmarked GPIO pins are standard, but those that have a value in parentheses are GPIO pins that can follow special protocols. If in doubt, use one of the standard GPIO pins. 3v3 pins supply 3.3 volts of electricity, and 5v supply 5 volts with an amperage that makes up whatever the Pi is not using to function. Ground pins are also known as 0v because they are used to return current. Later we will learn how circuits work and how these pins can be used for various functions.

GPIO pins are essentially binary switches that can be in one of two positions- off or on (also known as low or high). The pin can either be sending an electrical signal (1) or not sending a signal (0).

**Wiring to the Pi**

Circuits are made up of wires and components such as transistors, resistors, LEDs, sensors, and more. A circuit will generally make a loop starting at a pin on the RPI, connecting to the components, and then ending at another pin. Connecting the wires to the pins requires soldering, but soldering is messy and semi-permanent. For testing, you'll want to buy a breadboard and RPI ribbon cable, so that way you will be making connections on the breadboard instead of directly on the Pi. Some starter kits come with a breadboard already, but if it does not or you bought your RPI separately then you need to also purchase these extra parts online. Buying a simple RPI 3 breadboard and ribbon cable combo will alleviate the need for you to buy a soldering kit, and it will also ensure that you can reuse components from your projects over and over. The ribbon cable is not essential so long as your kit came with pin wires, which are wires that fit snugly over GPIO pins as to make a solderless connection.

Understanding how breadboards work is critical to digital engineering with microcontroller devices such as the RPI or Arduino. Because power flows through GPIO pins, beginners often make the mistake of frying their RPI through bad circuits. If you do not first understand how power flows there is a greater chance of something going wrong. Observe the sample breadboard below.

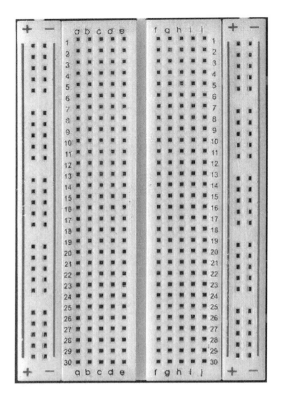

Breadboards typically have 4 sections from left to right. First, a positive and negative column. Then, a section of columns a-e (we used a-c as a smaller scale example). Then another section of lettered columns. Finally, another section of positive and negative. Rows are number incrementally as they go down. Long pieces of metal run vertically up the positive and negative columns supplying power, and short metal bars run horizontally through each numbered letter row. See the metal runs in the edited image below.

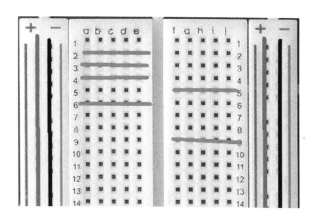

Therefore, you can insert bare wire leads or component parts into the holes and circuits can be made. Consider this simple LED circuit made with a 9v battery

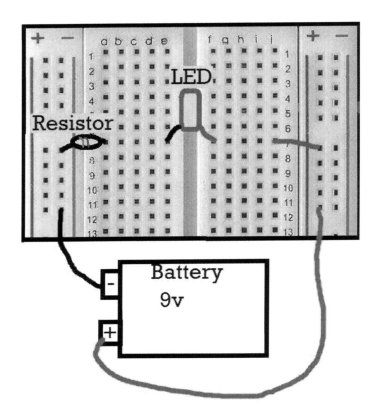

Notice how the current starts at the negative terminal of the battery. It travels to a hole on the breadboard that supplies power up and down that line. A resistor has one end in this power line, so the power travels through it and the current is reduced (resisted) by the component to a level safe for the LED. The other end of the resistor travels into 7A, and the power travels to 7E to be picked up by the red LED. It lights up, and the return current travels from 7F to 7J to be transferred to a positive power run. Lastly, the remaining current returns to the battery and cycle continues lighting up the LED until the battery runs out.

**Powering a LED with GPIO**

When using your RPI, though, it can potentially serve as a power source for the electronics.  Use the wire pins in your kit, solder wires, or attach them to a breadboard in this fashion:

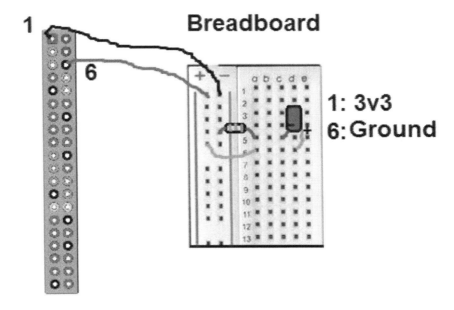

1
**Breadboard**
6
**1: 3v3**
**6: Ground**

We use a resistor that matches the LED we are trying to power here. In a starter kit there should be a matching set, but if you are buying parts manually you will need to do research about LEDs and how to match a resistor to it that will limit the power enough. Power flows continuously from the 3v3 pin, it travels to the resistor, to the negative lead of the LED, out the positive lead and into the positive rail, and then the power finally returns to ground on the RPI.

This is a simple circuit that will power an LED, but the beauty of microcontrollers is that current can be interfaced with via software as well. Due to this, we can control when the LED is on and off with a few lines of code.

The RPI uses Python heavily, and that is the language with which we can control GPIO pins. If you do not know Python do not worry, because we will provide the code below. First set up a very similar circuit to the one above.

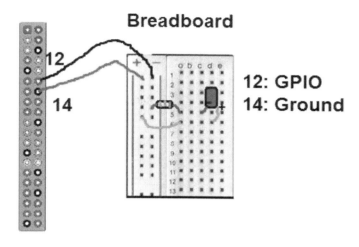

# Breadboard

**12: GPIO**
**14: Ground**

Current does not flow continuously from GPIO pins, instead, current only flows when it is turned on with code. Open a terminal by clicking the button on the menu at the top (it looks like a computer screen). The black windowed terminal appears and waits for your input. We want to create a Python program, so we must write the code with the nano application. Type "nano LED.py" to start editing a new file. Type the following code:

```
#!/usr/bin/python

import RPi.GPIO as GPIO

GPIO.setmode(GPIO.BCM)

GPIO.cleanup()
```

```
GPIO.setwarnings(False)

GPIO.setup(18, GPIO.OUT)

GPIO.output(18, GPIO.HIGH)
```

Press ctrl+x to save and quit the nano application. It will return to the terminal screen. We can run our newly created Python code by entering the command "python LED.py". The code runs all the way through, setting GPIO18 (pin 12) to HIGH mode which powers the LED. To turn the LED off we have to create a new file with "nano LEDoff.py". Insert these commands:

```
#!/usr/bin/python

import RPi.GPIO as GPIO

GPIO.setmode(GPIO.BCM)

GPIO.cleanup()

GPIO.setwarnings(False)

GPIO.setup(18, GPIO.OUT)

GPIO.output(18, GPIO.LOW)
```

And run it with "python LEDoff.py". This time, GPIO18 is set to LOW state, which cuts the power to the LED and it turns off. Congratulations, you have powered a component with your Raspberry Pi! It didn't have to be an LED, though, as any electronic could take its place in the circuit. For example, you could be powering a motor in a hobby project, or a sensor, or anything else that uses electricity.

More advanced projects will require additional Python knowledge. It is advised that you learn Python basics and also basic GPIO code as well. With the right know-how, you can write software to control anything. There are even kits that can be bought online that come with sets of parts for creating various projects. Look into them if you want another GPIO challenge.

**Do's and Don'ts of Circuit Building**

As previously explained, working with electricity can be dangerous. Although the current supplied by the RPI is low enough to not hurt humans, the current could still break your devices if you hook something up wrong or miss-program them. Thus, you should heed a few cardinal rules of building circuits.

DO:

- Hook up circuits to components with the RPI OFF and unplugged.
- Handle the RPI and components in a static-free environment, or wear a static wrist strap.
- Use resistors to limit current to delicate electronics that could break if overloaded with power.
- Follow any circuit diagrams exactly and double-check your wiring.
- Use breadboards so parts can be reused and connected without soldering.
- Buy electronics kits made specifically for your RPI 3.

DON'T:

- Buy an electronics kit with foreign language instructions only.
- Build random circuits without understanding the flow of electricity through your components.
- Connect wires to the pins labeled "DO NOT CONNECT".
- Use an incorrect pinout diagram, such as the one that was made for the RPI 2.
- Allow external power sources above 5v to flow back into the GPIO pins, as it could fry the Pi.

# Project Ideas

With the RPI 3's small size and competent processing ability, there is a multitude of awe-inspiring projects that you can undertake. This section serves as a general guide to a few popular projects and ideas that you can follow with your RPI 3.

## Digital Picture Frame

Your Raspberry Pi 3 is so small that it can even be fit into a picture frame. Digital picture frames are devices shaped like picture frames that cycle through pictures that you upload to them. They are expensive to buy, but the $35 RPI 3 is amazingly cheap and can fulfill the computing requirements of the frame easily.

This project works best with Raspbian OS. Install it or use your existing configuration. Within the terminal, type "sudo apt-get install feh" to install slideshow software capable of cycling through photographs or images.

Create a new folder in your home directory on your Pi and fill it with images. Now open up the command line and start a slideshow with this command:

```
DISPLAY=:0.0 XAUTHORITY=/home/pi/.Xauthority /usr/bin/feh
-q -p -Z -F -R 60 -Y -D 15.0 /picturesfolder
```

Obviously replacing "picturesfolder" with the name of the folder you created. The Pi will begin cycling through all of the pictures in your folder. Instead of typing that command every time you want to start the slideshow, though, we can create a script that automatically does it. Do "sudo nano start.sh" and type "#!/bin/bash" as the first line, and the above command as the second line. Save the file and exit. Make the file executable by typing "sudo chmod +x start.sh". Now you can run the file at any time within the directory by only typing "./start.sh".

Now that the software side of things is set up, we need to build the picture frame. Purchase a 3rd party RPI screen from any reputable dealer, and then find a picture frame to match the size. If you cannot find one that is exactly the screen size you can always make one out of wood or custom order one online. Connect the screen to the Pi, ensure everything works, and then mount everything in the picture frame. The electronics may have to poke out the back of the frame for everything to fit. Be creative in your placement of everything. Finally, mount the completed picture frame on the wall and plug it in. Start the slideshow and now you have a neat dynamic piece of art.

A related popular project that is based on this same concept is the "magic mirror" RPI. The magic mirror is a screen mounted behind a 1-way mirror. The brightness of the screen shows through the mirror and can thus be made to look as though the mirror is magic. You can have a slideshow on the mirror, or you could have it tell the temperature and weather. It just goes to show how versatile RPI projects can be.

**Make any TV "Smart"**

Older (and cheaper) televisions are often of the same image quality as 1000 dollar ones, but the biggest difference between the two is that the more expensive televisions have computers built-in that allow for "apps" such as Netflix, Hulu, and Amazon Prime Video. The $35 RPI 3 has the ability, however, to turn any TV with an HDMI port into a "smart" TV with technology on-par with the most expensive of brands.

Smart TV's have computers built-in, and these computers often run customized versions of Android. While Android is somewhat compatible with our RPI hardware, there exist better alternatives for media playback that take better use of the RPI's specific functionality. Moreover, a few apps like Netflix are not available for ARM systems, but free alternatives exist that outperform even paid streaming services.

Installing OpenELEC (Open Embedded Linux Entertainment Center) onto the bootable microSD card will give you an environment that allows for easy streaming playback. Download either the OpenELEC image from earlier in the book or NOOBS and write/copy to the microSD. Install OpenELEC in the same way you installed Raspbian.

Insert the microSD into your Pi and boot into OpenELEC. Use your mouse and keyboard to follow on-screen prompts setting up your network and other settings. Finally, you will be greeted by the OpenELEC menu. At this point, you can plug in a USB drive containing music or videos and be able to watch them.

If your house contains a networked media server, the RPI running OpenELEC can tap into the streams as well and watch media stored on your server. Most people, though, take OpenELEC further, and they install repositories containing collections of movies, TV shows, and more that can be watched on-demand. How legal it actually is to stream movies and television shows is unknown. You should check your local and state laws before actually continuing because we do not condone illegal actions. Nonetheless, the process is explained below for educational purposes.

Navigate to the "System" tab, click on "File Manager". On the new window that appears click "Add source". A prompt will appear asking for a path. We will add a link to the "super repo", a repository containing a plethora of free movies and TV channels. Type http://srp.nu/ and click "Add". Enter the name as "Super Repo". Navigate back to the main menu, click "System" and then "Settings", finally "Add-ons". Click "Install from ZIP file" to be taken to a file browser.

Some OpenELEC installations will contain a folder called "Super Repo" by default; if you see it click it. If you do not have the folder, you can download it from the SR website (https://superrepo.org/get-started/), place the folder onto a USB drive, insert it into the Pi, and navigate to it with the file browser to install it.

Once you click on the folder, it will open to reveal a few more folders. Choose the folder name that correlates with your version of OpenELEC. When downloading, you should have seen a codename such as Isengard or Gotham that signifies which release of OpenELEC you are using. If in doubt, check back to your download source for OpenELEC. Click on the folder, then click "all". At last you will see a single ZIP file. Click it to start the repo Add-on installation.

When the process finishes, various add-ons will be installed that you can now enable. As an example, we will enable a few popular video add-ons that provide streams to blockbuster movies and television shows. Click on the "Video" tab, and then click "Add-ons". None will be displayed, but we can click "Get more" to show a list of the add-ons that we installed earlier. Scroll through the large list and find one you would like to enable, such as "Pheonix", "1Channel", or "Genesis". These "channels" are what give you links to various streams.

Back on the main screen, you can go to "Videos", then to "Add-ons" to access the content of them. You now have a supercharged. You can mount it on the back of your TV and suddenly your old "dumb" TV can now connect to the internet and download streams for you to watch. Check out the peripherals section for an IR module and remote that you can use to really make it a "TV" experience.

**Retro Pi**

Vintage game consoles such as the Atari 7800 and the NES were highly fun back when they were released. Playing those games now is terribly difficult, though, because most people have gotten rid of their old consoles or do not have the money to invest in expensive game cartridges. Luckily a software imitating methodology known as "emulation" was created to make computers act like older consoles, thus making the games playable on PC.

Emulation has advanced to the point now where PS2 and Wii games can run at HD resolutions on modest computing setups, and PS3 and Xbox 360 emulation does not seem too far off. Consoles that do not require intensive processing, such as the PlayStation or Nintendo 64 are entirely playable on even slower hardware, such as the Raspberry Pi. Because of the small nature of the Pi and its cheap price, many people turn their device into an emulation machine affectionately called a "Retro Pi".

The legality of downloading and playing games without owning them is dubious. Look into your country's laws on the act before downloading anything from the internet. We do not condone illegally downloading copies of games, but we do encourage you to play backups of games that you own on the Pi because that is perfectly legal.

Retro Pi setups are made easy through the alternate operating system with the same name as the project. On a different computer, download the image (https://retropie.org.uk/download/) and extract the file if it is compressed. Files with the .7z extension need another program 7-Zip (http://www.7-zip.org/) to be decompressed. Lastly, write the decompressed image to the microSD with Win32DiskImager.


Plug everything into the RPI 3 and supply power. Retro Pi, which is just a customized version of Raspbian, will boot into the "Emulation Station" application. Retro Pi will first show a menu where you must configure your keyboard keys. Press the buttons that it asks for, navigate to the bottom and press the button you assigned to "A" to confirm "OK".


After setup, you will come to the main menu of Retro Pi. If you have a wired Xbox 360 or PS3 controller, plug it into a USB port. Games are much easier to play with a gamepad, and even the Emulation Station menu can be used with a wired controller. Press the keyboard key you associated with "start", move down to "Configure Input", and press your configured "A" button. A prompt should recognize your controller, and you should press the "Home" (or "PS") button to begin configuring it. You will go through the input setup process again, but this time with your gamepad. Press "OK" with your gamepad's "A" (Xbox) or "X" (PS) button to confirm, and you can now navigate the Emulation Station much easier with the controller.


The OS is set up now, but it does not come with any games installed by default. To get games, you will need to plug in a flash drive to another computer. Games are stored in ROM files of various file types, and they represent digital backups of a video game. Backup up and playing your own games is perfectly 100% legal, and the process to backup different consoles is different, but you can do internet research to find a method that works best for you. Alternatively, you could download other people's backups of games they own. This is the part that could potentially be illegal depending on your state or country's laws. However, most console makers simply do not care about downloadable ROMs for their older consoles, and you can find copies in various places online.

Before downloading or making backups of the ROMs you want to play, you need to prepare the USB for use in Retro Pi. Make sure the USB is formatted (Computer, right-click, format), and create a new folder with the name "retropie". Remove the USB and plug it into your RPI 3. Wait a few minutes as the device automatically configures your USB. It is safe to remove when the access indication light stops flashing. Plug the drive back into your home computer.

Various websites (http://romhustler.net/, http://www.emuparadise.me/, www.freeroms.com/) have links to download game ROMs, and all you need to do is download the game ROM you want to play and extract the file (if it is compressed). Open back up your USB and you will notice that there are new folders with console names. Drag the ROMs you obtained into their respective console's folder. Safely remove the USB and put it back into the RPI. Depending on your configuration Retro Pi could attempt to copy over the ROMs to the microSD, which could take a while.

Nonetheless, you are almost ready to play emulated games on your Pi. Press start on your controller (or the keyboard button you assigned to it) and confirm "Quit" followed by "Restart Emulation Station". After it finishes, you will see all of the consoles that you have games available for. Go to a console, confirm, and then select a game to play. Your ROM will start playing. Congratulations on a successful setup!

For advanced options, press the "A" button when the game is launched. You can configure alternate controls, different emulators, or enhanced features with the menu that appears.

Enjoy playing your games. One thing to note is that to return to the main menu you can press Start + Select at the same time.

A dedicated hobbyist will undoubtedly want to take the project further, which you can read about in the next section.

## Creating an Arcade Cabinet

Because the RPI has GPIO pins, it is in a unique position for gaming. Arcade buttons can be wired into circuits and programmed to act as a controller for your games. You can build an arcade cabinet around the entire project to give it an authentic feel, and then use leftover GPIO pins to light up LEDs for the marquee. The project does not have to specifically be an arcade cabinet because you can fit the Pi just about anywhere. Consider fitting one into an old game console, or into your car. The Pi is small enough to fit inside of a Gameboy, even. For this project, though, we will be building a full-sized upright arcade cabinet.

As for the parts you need, it depends on how in-depth you want the project to become. You can purchase a television screen for the monitor, individual buttons and joysticks to create a custom gamepad, or you can just build a wooden frame around your existing Retro Pi setup.

Some websites offer kits (http://www.retrobuiltgames.com/the-build-page/porta-pi-arcade-kit/) that have everything you need, such as wood, buttons, joysticks, and a monitor. These are recommended for true enthusiasts.

Alternatively, you can buy actual arcade switches online individually (https://www.ultimarc.com/goldleaf.html). The RPI can handle as many inputs as GPIO pins it has remaining, so plan out your build before buying too many parts.

The entire build process would span another entire book, so we will condense down the steps to the most important bits here:

1. Obtain all needed parts.  This includes-
   a.  Panels of wood, hardware, and power tools to assemble it all.
   b.  Your RPI 3 with a breadboard and plenty of wires.
   c.  A monitor and way to power it.
   d.  All the buttons you want to be included.
2. Lay out your buttons in an acceptable configuration. Trace the buttons onto your control panel and drill out holes for the buttons to sit in.
3. Cut and assemble the rest of your arcade cabinet.
4. Remove any electronics, and either paint or stain the wood.  Add a clear coat for a smooth surface.
5. Place the monitor into the cabinet along with the control panel and RPI 3 with Retro Pi.
6. Wire the buttons to the GPIO pins and write the Python program to control them all.

7. Plug everything in together and configure your new controls in Emulation Station.

8. Enjoy your home-built arcade-machine.

Every builder's arcade cabinet will be unique, and thus every wiring scheme will also be unique. Here is an example of how you can wire everything together.

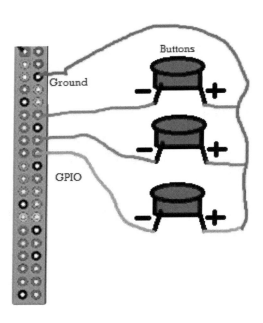

In this simplified diagram, power flows from GPIO ports into the negative terminal of a button. The circuit cannot be completed unless the button is pushed down, in which case the current travels back to ground and the RPI will register the result. Note that the buttons we used for the example are only one type of button. Some have more terminals, and some are wired differently. Follow any wiring instructions that come with your kit or components. Nonetheless, the Pi can be programmed to translate completed circuits such as the ones made above into button presses as though it were a controller.

There is an application that simplifies this process (so we don't have to learn more complicated Python). Plug in a keyboard to the RPI while Retro Pi is running and press F4 (or shift F4). You also need to connect the Pi to the internet, so do this with a wired LAN cable.

Next, type these commands:

mkdir mkjoystick

cd mkjoystick

wget https://github.com/digitalLumberjack/mk_arcade_joystick_rpi/releases/download/v0.1.4/install.sh

If the command requires root, reface it with "sudo". If it claims wget is not installed, use "sudo apt-get install wget". Now enter the final command.

sudo sh ./install.sh

The application will install and provide you with more commands that allow you to setup your controller. Initialize it with:

sudo modprobe mk_arcade_joystick_rpi map=1

Now the program will be constantly getting input from the GPIO pins. If you returned to the Retro Pi screen and set up a new controller, it would recognize the GPIO pins as a device. However, the program still requires you to run it with the terminal every time the Pi is started up. We can create a script to start automatically, though, to alleviate this need. Type this command:

sudo nano /etc/modules

A text file will open in nano. Type "mk_arcade_joystick_rpi", then press ctrl+x to save and quit. Create another file:

sudo nano /etc/modprobe.d/mk_arcade_joystick.conf

With the text "options mk_arcade_joystick_rpi map=1".

Safely reboot your RPI (shutdown −r now) and Emulation Station will start up again. Configure a new gamepad with your custom GPIO controller. Now, you have built a classic arcade cabinet with new technology. If you have any problems getting input to work, check out the applications help page (https://github.com/recalbox/mk_arcade_joystick_rpi/blob/master/README.md). Furthermore, there might be a few people on the internet with the same problems as you, so just search the difficulty that you are having online.

Creating an arcade cabinet is a laborious project, but also one that has a high payoff when you can sit back and enjoy your work. Successfully building the cabinet takes a skilled hobbyist or one with unmatched dedication. Feel proud for completing one.

**Home Automation**

The RPI 3 is a small and powerful device. It can fit just about anywhere, which means that just about anything can hold a computer to gain new features and functions. Home automation has historically been an expensive dream for most people. But since the RPI 3 is only $35 dollars, automating any item in your house is within reach.

Because of the endless possibilities, we cannot go through an entire project built guide. But any item in your house can become automated when you control it with an RPI. Installing Windows 10 IoT gives your Pi programming functionality available from Microsoft's Visual Basic Studio.

You can then control GPIO pins on the Pi to interact with your household appliances.

For example, you can wire an on/off switch to a table lamp and connect the circuit to the RPI.  With a little programming, you can control the lamp.  Add extra sensors for more features- like a clapper to turn the light on/off, or a daylight sensor so it automatically comes on at night.

Another idea is to attach a servo motor onto the Pi and mount it on your front door.  Control the servo with code and have it turn the lock on the door.  Now you have an automated front door that you can lock or unlock from anywhere by sending commands to the Pi.

As it is evident, home automation can be a fun project for your RPI.  Combine the computer with just about any aspect of your home to create an interconnected network of smart home devices that can be controlled from your computer.

# Accessories for the Pi

As popular as the RPI is, there are also plenty of 3$^{rd}$ party add-ons and peripherals that increase functionality or make the computer more useful.  None of them are essential to using the RPI, but most of them enable new projects or experiments, and some just make the computer easier to use.  We list a few of the most interesting peripherals below and their use.

The most well-known 3$^{rd}$ party peripheral sellers are AdaFruit, Element14, Make, and PiHut.  Buying from any of those dealers generally means you will receive high quality products.  Although cheaper alternatives exist, there is always the risk that you will buy a foreign piece of junk or something that has poor build quality.  Avoid used accessories from eBay, and predominantly stay with the more reputable dealers.

## Starter Kits

Every reseller has their own version of a "starter kit".  Some contain bare essentials such as an RPI 3 and a power source.  Others, though, such as AdaFruit's starter kit have everything you need to get up and going experimenting with digital electronics.  It has an RPI 3 with microSD (NOOBS preinstalled), a breadboard and GPIO ribbon cable, and a case with fitting power supply.  For electronics, it comes with various LEDs, buttons, resistors, and other components- along with enough wires for a variety of projects.


For the person wishing to get an RPI for educational fun, the AdaFruit starter kit is the perfect buy.  More curious learners can get a kit with more components, such as the CanaKit starter kit.


Lastly, there are starter kits that do not include the Pi.  Their purpose is to give you every component you need to do a certain project, or give you a wide array of sensors and electronics to play with.  Camjam has one such kit (alternatively, try this one) that comes with temperature sensors, LEDs, PIR sensors, and more.  Instead of buying parts individually, pick up an electronics kit that has everything you need to get your project going.


**On-Off Switch**


Because the RPI is always on if power is supplied, it creates an issue for a few hobby projects.  There are a few solutions for adding in on/off switch functionality, but most of them involve GPIO pins and scripts.  If our project is already using GPIO pins this could be a problem. But <u>PiSupply's On/Off switch</u> solves this issue by creating a daughterboard that handles power delivery.

You power the board like normal but place the PiSupply switch in-between the power source and the RPI. Power can be interrupted by cutting the switch off, or you can turn the Pi on by pushing it to the on position. The board works well when you safely shutdown (sudo shutdown –h now) your computer, as it automatically switches to "off" when it is safe to do so.

The switch comes as a kit that you can solder, but some sites sell it as a ready-to-go unit. Definitely include it in your hobby projects, because the RPI lacking an on/off switch is a puzzling design decision. Nonetheless, you can add the feature in for a low price with the custom accessory.

**Real-Time Clock**

The absence of a CMOS battery for time-keeping means that every time your Pi shuts down it is unable to update the current time. Desktop and laptop computers have a small battery that keeps the time even when the computer is powered off and unplugged, but the RPI forwent the inclusion of an RTC to save you money and space.

An RTC can be added in, however, that attaches to GPIO pins and allows for time-keeping even when the RPI is unplugged.  If your project requires time, but you do not want to have to set the time every instance the Pi is powered on, definitely include an RTC accessory.  Alternatives work just as well and only require a few GPIO pins to use.

**Audio Expansion Board**

A great project for an RPI is converting an old analog clock into a digital "smart" clock.  HDMI audio is nice, but sometimes we need a few more outputs.  This expansion board has 3.5mm ports, S/PDIF digital out, microphone ports, and more all running at studio-level 24 bit quality. Audiophiles need not worry about the sounds coming from the Pi anymore when this peripheral is added because the GPIO-pluggable board will produce an accurate sound at a decent price.

## GPIO Peripherals

Working with breadboards is a fun way to have a solderless experience with digital electronics. However, without a certain kind of cable, it is impossible to attach a wire to the Pi directly without soldering. A "breakout" board such as AdaFruit's Pi T-Cobbler Plus contain a device you attach to the GPIO pins and send to a breadboard with a ribbon cable. This ensures that nothing is ever edited on the RPI, protecting it from accidental danger.

Advanced projects with a lot of inputs may potentially run out of GPIO pins before the project is complete. With a GPIO expansion board, this will never be a problem because even more pins can be added to suit your needs. The specific board linked above is unique in that you can supply 5v power to it separately. The Pi can still control the pins like normal, but the power draw will not inadvertently strain the RPI with all of the extra pins.

Finally, digital electronics can be made easier with a Digital I/O Expander. This product by SparkFun plugs directly into the GPIO pins. On the expansion board are a variety of LEDs, switches, inputs, outputs, and relays. When setting up circuits, these parts do not need to be included in the diagrams, because they are "hard wired" into the Pi now. The software can be combined to create complicated circuits easily. It is a must for anybody working with GPIO pins frequently.

**Camera**

There is an interface on the Pi that many people will never use. You must attach hardware to it via a ribbon cable, but only one official add-on is supported by the board. The RPI Camera (https://thepihut.com/collections/raspberry-pi-accessories/products/raspberry-pi-camera-module) is a 5 or 8 megapixel camera that plugs directly into the Pi board. You can then use it within various operating systems for plenty of different tasks (note that there are special steps to enable the device within Raspbian).

You can take high-resolution video/pictures with the camera and save them to the SD card, or you can create a web server and stream the camera feed as though it were a security camera. Possible hobby projects include:

- A "nanny cam" hidden camera tucked away in a stuffed animal.
- Create a piece of clothing (suit jacket?) with the camera hidden behind a button.  Enjoy taking video as James Bond.
- Create a baby monitor that sends you snapshots of your child's room every 10 minutes.
- Attach the Pi to your front door so you can know who is knocking without opening it.
- Build a security system of interconnected Raspberry Pi computers with cameras for cheaper than the cost of a real system.
- Attach your Pi camera to a model rocket or balloon and get a view of your neighborhood as it goes up.
- Attach the camera to a pet via a body harness to see what they are up to when you are not around.

For nighttime projects, the Noir V2 is a supported camera that uses infrared lenses to enable night vision.  Overall, the total number of projects possible with a camera peripheral is astounding.


**Television Peripherals**


As popular as the "Smart" TV RPI project is, there are also plenty of peripherals to enhance the experience.  After creating an OpenELEC TV station and plugging it into your TV, the device has nowhere to rest besides on a table or hanging by the cord.  The OmniVESA mount solves this issue by providing a way for your RPI to bolt on the back of your television.

You can mount the RPI directly with the mounting holes on the PCB, or you can use some cases with mounting holes to attach it to the back of your TV.  It works by attaching itself to the holes many televisions have for VESA mounts, and it converts the Pi's mounts to be compatible.  Your smart TV project now looks incredibly professional.

Lastly, you can attach IR peripherals to the Pi's GPIO pins to add to an IR receiver.  Combined with a remote, this allows you to forgo a keyboard and mouse in favor of a more traditional television viewing experience.  The tutorial in the link tells how to program our OpenELEC installation to accept input from the IR remote, or potentially a universal remote.  Overall this peripheral set makes our DIY tv project into one that looks highly professional.

**Cases**

There is no shortage in custom cases for the RPI.  Because the general form factor of the RPI has not changed much between models, they are almost all compatible with each other.  The RPI 3 has extra USB ports compared to a few earlier models, though, so purchasing a case requires researching whether the top two ports will be blocked or not.

The benefits of using a case are numerous. They protect from drops, so your Pi project can possibly survive a small fall or impact. Moreover, cases protect the delicate electronics from static shock. The bare board is certainly aesthetically pleasing as far as circuit boards go, but accidently touching it without a properly grounded static strap has the chance of frying the board entirely. With a case, your electric charge will be nullified and not travel through the circuit board. Lastly, cases can be used to weather-proof your projects. Some hobby constructions and outdoor plans expose the RPI to the elements. A sudden drop of water due to rain might ruin your computer, but adding a case obviously lowers this risk. Overall, you should be using in most scenarios for your Pi.

Cases can be purchased almost anywhere online. Because cases cannot harm the Pi in any way (unless it is metal and poorly made), it typically does not matter where you acquire one from. AdaFruit, PiHut, Element14, and even random sellers on eBay will all have cases of varying qualities and styles. Choose one that fits your project, your budget, and your personal taste.

## Screens

Choices for screens are probably more varied than the choices for cases. Any HDMI device can be used for displaying the RPI's image- including televisions, PC monitors, and tablet touch screens. The high number of screen manufacturers mean there are plenty of options available from a plethora of dealers. Quality screens come at a premium price, though, so be prepared to spend a lot of money for a reliable and good looking panel. Try to purchase from a reputable seller, also, so you can read reviews and find a product that performs well.

Screens vary between RPI sized touchscreens to e-ink panels only capable of outputting black and white. Most of the screens need to be powered externally, so take this into consideration when putting together a project. It is possible to find a screen that can also be powered from 5v, which means you can use a Pi power supply to turn it on. Finally, some screens and cases can be sold together as a set, meaning you can have an all-in-one solution for using your Raspberry Pi. Keep an eye out for interesting visual solutions for computing with your RPI 3.

## Advanced Circuits with the RPI 3

Outputting electrical signals to the GPIO pins allows for LEDs, buzzers, fans, and more to be powered through Python code.  Highly useful, but GPIO pins are also used for input as well.  Some hobby projects are made more useful with sensors, such as if you were making a weather device.  The RPI would interface with sensors like barometers, a GPS, and a thermometer through the GPIO pins.  These components need to send data back to the Pi in order for them to be useful, and this tutorial will show how it is done.

We will use a DS18B20 temperature sensor and a 4.7 kilo-ohm resistor (use this site to match color bands).  This sensor is compatible with the GPIO pins in the Pi, and some starter kits come with it included.  It can also be acquired online as an individual component.  Follow the circuit diagram below to understand how to set it up.

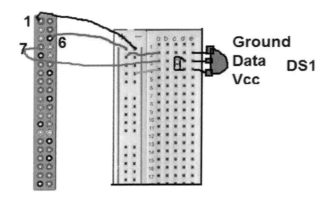

Power flows from the 3v3 GPIO to the Vcc pin on the thermometer. It powers the component and flows out of the ground into the ground pin. Data is transferred to pin 7, which is GPIO4. The resistor ensures that the data pins get power but not too much.

To receive input from the new sensor, we have to enable it first. In a terminal (Raspbian), type "sudo nano /boot/confit.txt" to start editing the boot file. At the bottom, add a new line "dtoverlay=w1-gpio". Save and quit with ctrl+x. Restart your computer (shutdown –r now). Open the terminal again and type the following lines:

sudo modprobe w1-gpio

sudo modprobe w1-therm

And the sensor is now on and collecting data. With a little Python script, we can see the input. Create a new

Python file with "nano temp.py". Enter the following lines (program courtesy of CircuitBasics):

```
import os, glob, time

os.system('modprobe w1-gpio')

os.system('modprobe w1-therm')


base_dir = '/sys/bus/w1/devices/'

device_folder = glob.glob(base_dir + '28*')[0]

device_file = device_folder + '/w1_slave'


def read_temp_raw():

    f = open(device_file, 'r')

    lines = f.readlines()

    f.close()

    return lines


def read_temp():

    lines = read_temp_raw()
```

```python
while lines[0].strip()[-3:] != 'YES':
    time.sleep(0.2)
    lines = read_temp_raw()
equals_pos = lines[1].find('t=')
if equals_pos != -1:
    temp_string = lines[1][equals_pos+2:]
    temp_c = float(temp_string) / 1000.0
    temp_f = temp_c * 9.0 / 5.0 + 32.0
    return temp_c, temp_f


while True:
        print(read_temp())
        time.sleep(1)
```

Press ctrl+x and save the file. Now type "python temp.py" to start the program and start receiving input every second. Move the sensor around and see the input change. Lastly, quit the program with ctrl+c.

Advanced circuits with the Pi will use layouts similar to the one we made. Power will flow through the breadboard, and there will be GPIO pins that carry data back instead of just electricity.

As you create advanced circuits, you will either create your own or follow diagrams that are created with a special notation. So far the wiring diagrams in this book were a custom shorthand created for your readability. But when you buy a kit or follow a tutorial you will usually be given a schematic to refer to. Take for instance this simple diagram.

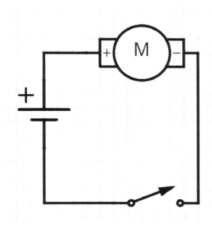

The symbols schematics correlate with various components in a circuit. The horizontal lines above are a power source, such as a batter, or possible the 3v3 line on the

RPI. Power flows through the negative side and reaches a switch, signified by a line that is broken. When the switch is closed, power can continue flowing. In this circuit, it would continue to a motor that would spin. Your hobby project might have a different load there, such as an LED or a temperature sensor. The power flows back to the source, thus completing the circuit and allowing the components to operate.

You can build your own schematics through a few different online programs, or you can sketch it out on pieces of paper. Learning what each symbol is and how to recognize it can be a chore, so it helps to keep a guide handy. If you can read complicated schematics, you can build anything with your RPI.

# Raspberry Pi Tips and Tricks

After playing around with your RPI 3 enough, eventually, you will become a master. There are still a few tips and tricks to help you out with your hobby projects and experiments, and this section will list a few of them.

## SSH

The typical Pi setup contains a monitor attached so you can program or run code on the machine. For projects that leave the Pi outdoors, though, you might not always have the power to have a screen plugged in. Furthermore, it is much easier to interact with your Pi when you don't have to unplug your current computer setup to give a screen to the Pi. With a tool called SSH, the Pi does not need a screen at all because you can use another computer attached to the same network to see what is on the RPI.

You still need a screen when initially setting up a Pi, because you need to enable SSH in a menu of Raspbian. In a terminal type "sudo raspi-config". Scroll down the menu options and enable SSH. Quit the configuration and type "ifconfig" into a terminal. Write down your IP address, which should be listed under "inet addr". Restart the computer to save your config changes.

Now, you can use a home computer, cell phone, or any other device on the same network as the RPI. In Windows, the program PuTTY (http://www.putty.org/) allows you to connect via SSH; download and install it. Within the application, type the IP address of the RPI and click "Open" to connect. A command prompt window will open and ask for the username and password of the Pi. After authenticating yourself, you will now be interfacing directly with the RPI as if you plugged in a screen. You can run terminal commands by just typing them into the command prompt, and they surely will run on the Pi.

Use SSH to check data from anywhere, or interface with the RPI without having to use a screen. It is a useful tool that is worth enabling.

**Installing New Software in Raspbian**

The default programs are suffice for menial tasks, but new programs are sometimes needed. Within a terminal, type "sudo apt-get install programname" replacing the placeholder text with the program of your choice. A few possible program names are "chromium-browser", "gimp", or "Tetris".

The newer version of Raspbian makes the process even easier because you do not need to use the terminal. Access the Pi Store application and click on programs to install them. If you do not have the Pi Store program, install it with "sudo apt-get install pistore".

**Overclocking the RPI**

Advanced RPI users can squeeze extra performance out of the tiny minicomputer by overclocking the processor on the Pi. Overclocking is when you run a chip at a higher frequency than intended. It will give better performance, but also output more heat. Because the Pi has no fan or heatsink on its chips, overclocking will increase the heat output very much- the board could potentially fry itself if it is overclocked too high.

Before attempting to overclock, know that it is a dangerous act that should only be done by people that know what they are doing. Secondly, you should add a heatsink and fan to the Pi to decrease the heat output. Lastly, edit the "config.txt" file in "/boot" and change the "arm_freq" value to over/underclock the device. 1400 is a decently high value, and it is not recommended to go any higher without a serious cooling implementation. After rebooting the machine it will run at the new clock speed and so long as the heat is under control the Raspbian OS should be relatively stable.

Overclocking is dangerous, but it could make your project much better. For example, the Retro Pi may struggle on intensive games, but overclocking would increase performance just enough to make them playable. Only overclock if you understand the risks, though, because overclocking too high can turn the RPI into an unusable brick.

# Conclusion

The Raspberry Pi 3 mini computer is an amazing device. In addition to being the size of a credit card, it also has enough processing power to replace an entire computer. For DIYers, hobbyists, and digital engineers, the RPI is an interesting device because of the GPIO pins that is contained. A multitude of projects are available, and the number of things that can be built with a Pi 3 are limitless.

Conclusively, the RPI 3 is a fantastic improvement over its predecessors. Furthermore, it has better build quality than other SoC computers, and also more 3$^{rd}$ party peripherals and community support. Playing with a Pi can teach you about programming, digital electronics, and electricity as you build circuits and discover how components work.

The relatively cheap nature of the Pi means that building your own devices often saves you money. Turning a "dumb" TV into a "smart" one only needs the $35 computer, and building a Wi-Fi enabled hidden camera to watch your house can be done for under $50.

The Raspberry Pi fosters creativity and provides children and adults alike with an outlet for learning.  Continue experimenting with your RPI 3 and have fun being creative.

# Other Books by Timothy Short

Linux: The Quick Start Beginners Guide

Wordpress: Beginner to Pro Guide

Shopify: Beginner to Pro Guide

Passive Income: The Ultimate Guide to Financial Freedom

Project Management: Beginner to Professional Manager and Respected Leader

Blockchain: The Comprehensive Guide to Mastering the Hidden Economy

All available via amazon.com

Made in the USA
San Bernardino, CA
27 November 2016